T0015573

ETYMOLOGIES

© Copyright Walter Ancarrow, 2023. All rights reserved.

Cover art and design by Peter Maher Salib

Interior design by Walter Ancarrow

Cover typeface: DIN Condensed
Interior typeface: Garamond Premier Pro, DIN Condensed, Beirut

Library of Congress Cataloging-in-Publication Data

Names: Ancarrow, Walter, 1988- author.
Title: Etymologies / Walter Ancarrow.

Description: Oakland, California : Omnidawn Publishing, [2023] | Summary:
"Etymologies conceives of language as process, rather than language as
fixed history. These poems build imaginative mini-worlds of possible
word-use. They create a playful quasi-reference work that flips standard
assumptions about word origins—mainly that such origins exist. The text
questions the intent of any writer using an etymology to prove a
specific meaning. In so doing, Etymologies pays particular attention to
relation: of the cultures and conflicts, migrations and hegemonies that
create our words, words that are furthered by us, who in speaking push
them into the future"-- Provided by publisher.

Identifiers: LCCN 2022057661 | ISBN 9781632431134 (trade paperback)
Subjects: LCGFT: Poetry.
Classification: LCC PS3601.N415 E89 2023 | DDC 811/.6--dc23/eng/20221207
LC record available at https://lccn.loc.gov/2022057661

Published by Omnidawn Publishing, Oakland, California
www.omnidawn.com
10 9 8 7 6 5 4 3 2 1
ISBN: 978-1-63243-113-4

ETYMOLOGIES

WALTER ANCARROW

OMNIDAWN PUBLISHING
OAKLAND, CALIFORNIA
2023

FOR PETER
لبيتر

INTRODUCTION

Etymology—the study of the origin of words—has had many lives. In Plato's *Cratylus*, Hermogenes took the position that nothing but local or national convention determines which words are used to designate which objects. He recognized that language was a set of conventions or, what Ludwig Wittgenstein called, "devices." The same names could have been attached to quite different objects, and the same objects given quite different names, so long as the users of the language agreed upon their usage. He seems to have been a literalist.

Cratylus took the opposite position. He believed that names were embodiments of the object's essential identity, and that if you referred to something by a name other than its natural one, you failed to refer to it. In Plato's dialogue, Socrates's own position has engendered much discussion among scholars without leading to any consensus, as he seems to either side with Cratylus or mock him or perhaps both, all while not quite fully rejecting Hermogenes. Did the ancients encode each word with meanings, which are waiting to be unlocked by a future reader? What stories does the changing usage of a word tell us? What has shaped their usage?

In *Etymologies*, Walter Ancarrow writes up his findings of words, such as *caravan*, *pumpernickel*, and *sequoia*. Out of his choices the reader will sense a moiré pattern of associations emerging, at once particular and elusive. We seem to see it, but we cannot fix it in our mind's eye. Ancarrow combines extreme precision with a wild imagination. In a note at the end of the book, he writes: "The etymologies in this book are correct, though not necessarily complete, sometimes poetically so." And therein lies the magic of *Etymologies*. The author seems to have made nothing up, to have been, it would appear, coolly objective throughout the writing of each study of a word's origin. And yet, despite this claim, which I do not doubt, feelings and fancifulness emerge—like a swarm of genies freed from many bottles—at once impish, amatory, mysterious, provocative, funny, delightful, and dazzling.

—citation of **JOHN YAU**, judge of the 2021 Omnidawn Open Poetry Contest and author of *Genghis Chan on Drums*

ETYMOLOGIES
NOTE
ACKNOWLEDGMENTS

"You will know them by their fruits."
—Matthew 7:16

ahuakatl
aguacate
avocado

electric from Latin *electrum* from Greek *elektron*, "amber"; her necklace a slow
bug zapper

caravan from Arabic al-Qayrawan, the westernmost city of Islam. In its madrasa lies an atlas of lands beyond: asemic, incomprehensible, blank. Thoughts are the borders of words.

Mansur al-Hallaj: O Eternal One, how did you begin?

Allah:

Mansur al-Hallaj: O Answerer, I understand. Your origin is the space between what is definite (*al*, "the") and what can be named (*'lah*, "god"), *al 'lah*. By closing that gap do we come to know You as You.

In the Synagogue of the Logos, a rabbi interred the geniza, those sacred texts containing His unutterable name. In a distant land, *book* grew out of Proto-Germanic *bokiz*, the beech tree. In burying what is unsayable we allow it to take root and then tower over us.

pumpernickel from German *pumpern*, "to pass gas," and *Nickel*, "goblin," for its unpalatable properties—fart goblin, ass kraken, Puck of petarade, ghost of dinners past, bumyip, Poot the Magic Dragon, Zephyrus unzipped, Eurus of your anus, Boreas of the ass-burp, Notus of the not-me, riddle of the stinks, will-o'-the-whiff, Sirens but deadly, nereid of the nether burble, Pan's toot, the Vegetable Lamb of Fartary, flight of the Nachtkrapp, munchkin of the butt-scrunch, bansheesh, sniffrit, CHAOS WHO ENGULFED THE WORLD AND BROKE THE WINDS. Father, expel my inner demons.

Spanish *diablo*, Italian *diavolo*, English *devil*, French *diable*, Romanian *diavol*, Portuguese *diabo*—all from Latin *diabolus*

"They speak in tongues," said the monoglot Evangelical. "Drive them out of this land."

urbane from Latin *urbanus*, "belonging to the city, citified, refined." The city built a wall to guard against its antonyms: the uncouth, the uncultured. Soon even travelers ceased to plod its museums—the city's name not recalled on maps, its route inaccessible and at the tip of the tongue, its famed wall useless round a metropolis protected by its inability to be expressed in a living language.

What you have forgotten is that my matriarch is Greek *medousa*, the feminine *medein*, "to protect," which I do: granite cliffs too sheer for men to grope; a gravel path fleeing the king's keep; mother earth, our rock, with her fire inside.

But think of me as you wish, Perseus: a gorgon, Poseidon's, a water-snake afraid of water. If men like you do not say so to my face, it does not mean your hearts are not already stone.

dhowtus and then *dauþuz* and then *deaþ* and then *death* and then *onion* from Old French *oignon* from Latin *unionem*, "unity, one"; it is only when cut deeply that you learn what you thought was depth was mere repetition of surface, each clear pane of yourself opening to another exactly the same, out of which you will never view the real thing stark in the cold air, you who are wholly unoriginal: that cut, this cause of your tears

Brave, tourist, the five boroughs in search of a bagel and its legendary center. In Williamsburg they speak of Yiddish origins: *beygl*, after an antique *bougel*, "ring"; while Western heresiarchs counter that it was forged in Hell's Kitchen. Natives of Alphabet City only say "O" and point to a bodega. The markets are of little use: amid ziggurats of spice, men rave cryptically of an almighty Everything. In Turtle Bay they confuse torus with tortoise. The jewelers of Midtown warn of a curse: the bagel's center cannot be unbezeled without breaking its ring; the gluttonous, desiring the possibilities of empty space, devour the enclosing solid. Its missing center falls out, lost as a void among voids.

la la la *lute* from Old Occitan *laut* from Arabic *al ʿud*, "the wooden stick";
faster beat the rising waves, grumbled Vesuvius at the end of the anthropocene,
but who is here to keep time?

Before *paper* there was, it is said, pre-Egyptian *papyrus*, the sedge. Blown left or right, reeds made signs read by farmers: a famine, a flood, a sea change. Later men leafing through bulrush divined boats and baskets and songs about a basket used as a boat to carry a baby. Mothers weaved stories and bracelets. Thus word-of-mouth and handicraft articulate each other. Noting a star over the delta, an oracle wondered if the unwritten could leave its mark.

a bed song: *eorþe* of *ertho* of *er-*, our ur-*earth* ere our Eng its inging a *scribe*'s antecedent: *skribh*, "to scratch" into bark, stone, earth

:

scribes, like cartographers, turn the world into paper

:

philosophers spoke of liber mundi. in certain tomes one finds answers at the end

:

the Prophet could reject material reality. he who never learned to read

:

at the Mosque of the Booksellers, scholars publish works by burning them on windy days

:

the *Muqaddimah* tells all history in that all history is an introduction

:

there is no projection without distortion, as Mercator knew

:

cartographers, like scribes, turn paper into the world

map from Old French *mapemonde* from Medieval Latin *mappa*, "cloth," and *mundi*, "world"

"When folded such fabrics of space-time transpose orient with occident: antipodes touch, URAL MOUNTAINS labels an unnamed sea, Cairo's dawn sweeps San Francisco's brume, the qibla points everywhere, which is Mecca. When unfolded the world resumes its mundane form. Only the folded map is a holy text—its symbols unseen, its referent a thought with no edge."

—Muhammad al-Idrisi, commentary on *Kitab nuzhat al-mushtaq fi ikhtiraq al-afaq*

How inhuman, jungle bird, to see the forest from the greens; that the blues you soar within do not soar within you; that red is a red of heliconia and a dusk you choose to sail against; that yellowing is not of age, but first light on the hibiscus; that you outfly your shades.

You are like us like this: that we call you *toucan, tucan, tukana*, because it is how the Tupi heard your cries—and who of us have not been caged by what we've fleetingly said?

sequoia from a Cherokee source as unknown as its creator. In the wind the ancient body creaks like a door opening and closing. A spotted owl poses its famed question to the other side.

YOU, TOO, CAN DREAM!

clud
cloud

A fabulist told of null-country, a realm in the shadow of Tagalog *bundok*, mountain, which city-goers called the *boondocks*. These mountains drew zigzags along the sky as if signed by an illiterate. In their folds sheep slid from one valley-side to another, beads of abaci adding nothing of value. The flowers were meaningless because unsensed.

In another version it was not the mountains that were a wasteland but the city. Its depths harbored barbarian ships and argots, while the subway map to get there was clear only to those fluent in color-speak. Neon signs flashed on and off unsure of their decrees. Each alleyway ended in longing because you did not go down it.

In both the moral was the same: people between city and mountain are most unhappy. For them, meaning is always everywhere else.

taboo from Tongan *tabu*, the sacred, from Proto-Polynesian *tapu*, "not to be touched," and spread by unspeakable acts around the world:

an ambiguous Ms. in Missoula,
an areolaholic from Brest,
a prodder of cattle from Moola,
a swarm of bug-chasers from Pest,
a man with bedsores in Mansoura,
an omphalophile from Omsk,
a walid kebab'd in Gomorrah,
a Dick with his Harry in Tomsk,
a chai boy big-spooned in Lashkargah,
a Zoroassman from Tehran,
a chubby-chasee in Chahar Gah,
a wop with a WAP in Milan,
a black-Thai affair in Mueang Phuket.
Admit what you did in Nantucket.

Speak. Give breath to what leaves its cold impression, like footprints of the woolly *mammoth* stepping out of Mansi *manjont*, earth, from which we come but do not return—each of us given a sky burial, in that we shift the air when spoken of in reminiscence or are forgotten as fog on memory. Taking a keen wind as a lament for home I knew by its sting.

what we know of the body: that it comes from Old English *bodig*; that it
begins with lips parting and an exhalation of breath; that it ends in why; that
it is "otherwise of obscure origin"

eg begat *ek* begat *ic* begat *I*,

caught between an old name for myself

and a future expression

: . . . ?

: *They will call you* adamah, *the earthling, and* adamu, *the maker, and* Adam, *the man; and later, onomast and nomothete—each name signifying the changing nature of your nature. Come, let me show you: the tree of knowledge is the proto-language, whose branches grow everywhere and whose fruits bear on the tongue. Allow them to contort your mouth, mud-slinger, and explain yourself.*

: . . . ?

: *No matter that my tongue forks: you will either express yourself in your own terms in a language of your own make, and thus become illegible in your shifting sense. Or you will believe you are clay carved into an ideogram of His being: in a word, unchanging, because in His word. In which case, you will waste your life reading your face over and over again, and being sorry for the story it tells.*

The *ogre* looked at himself in the mirror, having been asked how he could look at himself in the mirror. In his face he faced all he had been called before: *ogre*, "monster," *orco*, "demon," *Orcus*: straight out of Hades. Identity a form of imitated subjugation, he resisted capture by squealing his name indecipherably to the townsfolk, whose hunt followed the natter of the village idiom.

black, "darkest color, a race," from Proto-Indo-European *bhelg*, "to glow," via a series of illuminated manuscripts, scientific enlightenments, and bright ideas

Homo sapiens, "wise man," coined by Carl Linnaeus who pinned down the trembly fig leaf of name. Note that *homo* comes from Latin ("man") and not Greek ("same"), which is why there are no *hetero sapiens* (cf. *false friend*).

inuksuk ("a cairn in the shape of a man") from Inuktitut *inuk*, "person," and *suk*, "false":

some stood motionless and turned the wild wild
some had names of lovers carved deeply inside
some when fallen made snow angels
some did always have a hole in them
some remained stone-faced in light of the moon
some in their fixity moved the stars
some were repurposed by a local witch
some at the brink never looked back
some marked the end of themselves
some guided no traveler
some became sundials and shadows encircled their days
some endured the years just to collapse under the touch of a bird

here be *dragons*: in the crumpled geography of a fata morgana disclosing their ulterior alp; in the reference work of a rainbow, catalog of their hoarded gems made radiant by the observer's eye; in the hatching of their eggs as phosphenes in fields of vision; in bestiaries that trace their evolution from Greek *derkesthai*, "to see, to see clearly"; in a word that taps a private sense for a public non-existence

For his last temptation, Saint Anthony journeys to the Palace of Zerzura where on the floor of its innermost courtyard an artist places the final tile in a mosaic'd caricature of a beloved prophet. Anthony reels.

THE ARTIST. Where does your *anger* stem?

ANTHONY. From an obscure northern dialect: *angra*, to grieve. Do you not hear the cries of those unlike you?

THE ARTIST. But where does your anger stem?

He gestures obscenely while Anthony considers the prophet. The more he thinks the more images he creates mentally, setting each one in a prior experience and each with a meaning to which he must submit lest they be senseless. In this way he serves the image, serves the mirror of the image, which multiplies as he reflects.

ANTHONY. Anger is an image-maker and I idolize my prophet. To love him truthfully is to become disillusioned. It is why I grieve.

Exit Anthony through the gift shop where in distress he knocks over a row of mugs on which are printed the mosaic, their broken pieces sending copies into the air.

sad from Old English *saed*, "sated, enough"

LOVE SONG OF *MOKÈLÉ-MBÈMBÉ* WHO "STOPS THE WATERS"

no river ever
touched the same me twice

but sorrow flows like the self
filling in
my selves that have been

boomerang from a language of the Dharawal aborigines, who will not return from where they never left *oolong* from Mandarin *wū-lóng*, "dark dragon"; downed by the knighted in an oral tradition

ma9aytu ila al-shar8 7alaman wa 6alabtuhu 5ajalan ma4hulan min al-3aja2ab al-dafina:[1]

zero, a relic of Latin *zephirum* of Arabic *sifr* of Sanskrit *sūnya*: "a desert, an empty place"

beyond conception, its emptiness vanishing when filled with the thought of its own

[1] "I went to the East dreamily and sought it timidly, astonished by the hidden wonders" in Arabizi

origami from Japanese *oru*, "to fold," and *kami*, "paper":

forgo
the note pad for the lily,
o frog

:

malign form
is grounded in flatness; a flap uplifts
mr. flamingo

:

of sex,
one enfolds breath in craft; notice, in the snow,
foxes

:

a sawn
self: ice sheets break a mirror-lake, halve
a swan

:

arcane:
how the mind foresees in pleats of rain
a crane

petunia from Portuguese *petum* from Paraguayan Guaraní *pety*, "tobacco"; like smoke, these are what we impose on them: in a vase, they fill the vase, whose figure resembles yours, you who gave them to me; when wreathed on doors we slam shut, they are the hookah rings of the caterpillar questioning who we are; wild, they spread shapelessly without an other to hold them; planted in a garden, their flared petals signal in the dark that someone once tucked them in a bed, too

NUDE DESCENDING A STAIRCASE

spiðra
spiþer
spiþur
spiþre
spither
spydyr
spider

A pilgrim on his way to Lake *Chad* will think the oasis a double-mirage, for its name comes from Kanuri *tsade*, "lake." On the edge of this Lake Lake at the end of the Desert Desert, he stands with his body twinned in the water, and wonders which of him is word and which object. The songs of the bathers, the lanterns making glyphs of the far shore, a pink conch-shard whose curve suggests the whole—these call out to him, and by their pull on his heart, he knows the standing him is word, and that the object to which all he refers is his reflected self, the one so easily scattered.

catamaran from Tamil *kattu*, "bind," and *maram*, "tree, wood"

:

sprig of copper leaf, the spangled sea is not your mother

yes, the world swirls away. an eye is a knot in a line of sight

oh look! sea spray—oops no, a spray of spruce...

for sure we are water, sapling; to be so bound yet still float

(thus in drowning we become more ourselves)

:

so what: I gave you life and moved on. look how you fountain with leaves

"The history of heretofore *society* is the history of *class*."

The history of *class* begins at Proto-Indo-European *kele*—to shout.

The history of *society* begins at Proto-Indo-European *sekw*—to follow.

History is the search for that original utterance echoing down the archives.

[misplaced index]

America, United States of
—its historical organizations
    contents, subjecting of, x
    subjects, ordering of, x
—its measuring systems
    Dewey decimal, x
        see also: decimal, placement of as Sisyphean boulder
    imperial, x
        see also: world, every inch of the
—its name
    Amerika, x
        see also: the silent *k* in acknowledgement
    Vespucci, Amerigo, x
        see also: Gothic *amalrich*, "work ruler"
            see: aptronym
—its paradox
    home, and yet my love of, x
—its vexillology
    blue, x
        see also: *remembered hills, those*
    red, x
        see also: hands, tomatoes stain these
    white, x
        see also: sea to shining sea c. 1823
            see: the sea wash white
            see: whitewash
                see: what!?
                see: whit, not a
                see, witness

FAMILY, FAMILIA, FAMULUS ("SERVANT, SLAVE")

blood ties &
blood bonds

I would tell you of my *home*, said the adult, but what I call it now was called *ham* in the past, and *haimaz* before that, and earlier a name held secret. We live between impermanences of language—building a home is settling on translation.

roquefort from the village of Roquefort on a wedge of blue hill flocked with cumuli; *emmental* from the eponymous Alpine valley whose hollows and gorges, inclines and cavities form a topographic model of its export; *manchego,* named after its mother-sheep grazing La Mancha's plains, encased in horizons so wide that like a rind they cannot be consumed; *gorgonzola,* toponym of a town near Milan: city of blue-veined marbles, olfactory labor, acquired taste; *feta* from Greek *pheta,* Italian *fetta,* Latin *offa,* "morsel"—a column of leftover culture-product crumbling with age

"How does my *jasmine* grow?" asked Harun al-Rashid.

The botanist answered: "Out of Middle Persian *yasamin*."

"Yet it is unfamiliar."

"The scent cannot be inferred from your previous airs and dissipates with the very breath used to describe it. But in thought it can be given form."

"When I speak of the caliphate's borders they will think I speak of the caliphate's borders, but I speak of the scent of jasmine: in flux, invisible, existing in my conceiving it."

"You speak of the caliphate's borders."

In perceiving *paradise* he began at *pairi–*, to go around, and so he went: to arbors loud with the shibboleth of parrots, which unclasped like a diary from their perch as he passed; then to the Statue of a Peacock in Flight eroded to an empty plinth by the rain; he rested in gardens of silphium and the compass rose where at last he found himself in a hidden recess, a cleft in his brain from which he could not go further, could not think through without looping back, comparison being a type of escape. Here he took no leave.

Not because paradise is everlasting but that it ends
in *–diz*, the act of building a wall.

The mind that shapes the *bumblebee*'s name out of onomatopoeic *bombeln* is in turn shaped by the name of the bumblebee, which comes to evoke in the mind afternoons of anab-e-shahi and beards entangled, his scent now as distant as the summer it sowed, ripe years in which we could not tell the bee from the bumble, and to which the bumblebee, in its briefness, paid no mind.

The time came to build a permanence for which was sought an *architect*, who formed all forms first in the mind. But which? To understand each form another was needed: the lines of a blueprint, the marks of an alphabet, the modeling of a diorama. These, too, took explanation: schools of thought to interpret the lines, a grammar police to stay on script, a rhetoric and its dictator to rally model citizens—while others tried to make sense of these in books full of diagrams, jargon, theoretical models, one of which said: "Beware the architect. The 'master builder' of the ancients cannot help but construct form on top of form when searching for an ideal, each layer obscuring the plain connection of things: as when two people, with a mere touch, know they could never formulate what they mean to each other."

To enter *Babel*, one must follow Hebrew *Babhel* on the way from Akkadian *bab-ilu*, the Gate of God—but only ruins remain of mankind's attempt to converse one on One. A shorter journey ends at Merriam-Webster, the monument of an heretical sect that attempted to define all of His creation. The orthodoxy noted its curious feature: a word's meaning is determined by how it is used in relation to other words, whose meanings are found likewise: the monument was built on no foundation. A search ensued for the loose word that, if pulled out, would cause indescribable destruction.

banana
banana

NOTE

The etymologies in this book are correct, though not necessarily complete, sometimes poetically so. Sources include: *The Oxford Dictionary of English Etymology*, *The Online Etymological Dictionary*, *Merriam-Webster*, *World Heritage Encyclopedia*, *The Penguin Dictionary of Curious and Interesting Numbers*, *Wiktionary*, and *Arabs: A 3000 Year History*, for the etymology of *caravan*.

ACKNOWLEDGMENTS

Some etymologies previously appeared in *POETRY* and *The Adroit Journal*.

There are many people to thank and I thank all of them for their love, support, friendship, and guidance. Special thanks to Cally Conan-Davies, who taught me that down under is also a perspective, and to Joey de Jesus, a storm and the shelter from it.

Walter Ancarrow lives in New York City and sometimes Alexandria, Egypt. *Etymologies* is his first book.

Etymologies
by Walter Ancarrow

Cover art and cover design by Peter Maher Salib

Interior design by Walter Ancarrow

Cover typeface: DIN Condensed
Interior typeface: Garamond Premier Pro, DIN Condensed, Beirut

Printed in the United States
by Books International, Dulles, Virginia

Publication of this book was made possible in part by gifts from
Katherine & John Gravendyk in honor of Hillary Gravendyk,
Francesca Bell, Mary Mackey, and The New Place Fund

Omnidawn Publishing
Oakland, California
Staff and Volunteers, Spring 2023

Rusty Morrison, senior editor and publisher
Laura Joakimson, co-publisher and executive director
Rob Hendricks, poetry & fiction, & post-pub marketing
Sharon Zetter, poetry editor & book designer
Jeffrey Kingman, copy editor
Liza Flum, poetry editor
Anthony Cody, poetry editor
Jason Bayani, poetry editor
Gail Aronson, fiction editor
Jennifer Metsker, marketing assistant
Sophia Carr, marketing assistant